SAN FRANCISCO'S *famous* SEA LIONS

Angel Bea Publishing

To Ash, Ali, Chrissy, Andrew, Kirby and
Jo Jo
—K.S.

For Aaron and Kat
—J.M.

Special thanks to Claudia Cornett, Ann
Bauer and The Marine Mammal Center
for their expertise and support.
—K.S. and J.M.

Text copyright © 2002 by Kat Shehata
Illustrations copyright © 2002 by Jo McElwee

First U.S. edition 2002

Publisher's Cataloging-in-Publication

Shehata, Kat.
  San Francisco's famous sea lions / by Kat Shehata ;
illustrated by Jo McElwee. - - 1st ed.
  p. cm.
  SUMMARY : Describes the history of California sea lions
at San Francisco's Pier 39 and incorporates sea lion facts
into the story of how The Marine Mammal Center rescues
sick and injured sea lions.
  Audience: Ages 8 - 12.
  ISBN 0-9717843-0-2

  1. Sea lions- -California- -San Francisco- -Juvenile
literature. 2. Wild life rescue- -California- -San
Francisco- -Juvenile literature. 3. San Francisco
(Calif.)- - Juvenile literature. 4. Sea lions.
5. Wildlife rescue. 6. San Francisco (Calif.).
I. McElwee, Jo. II. Title.

QL737.P63S44 2002   599.79'75
                              QB133-452

Printed in Hong Kong

This book was typeset in
Augustal, and Times BradleyHand ITC

The illustrations were done in acrylic and colored pencil

SAN FRANCISCO'S
famous SEA LIONS

KAT SHEHATA

illustrated by

JO MCELWEE

ANGEL BEA PUBLISHING

9504 Bainbrook • Cincinnati, Ohio 45249

www.angelbea.com

Why do so many sea lions live at Pier 39? In the winter of 1989, about 6 sea lions began **hauling out** regularly at this popular tourist attraction. That number dramatically increased in just a few weeks. By January of 1990, more than 150 **gregarious** sea lions had completely taken over one of the docks at Pier 39.

Prior to 1989, sea lions were only spotted occasionally at Pier 39. "K" dock was being renovated, so for a period of time there were no boats docked there. This left plenty of room for the sea lions to haul out undisturbed. Boat docks are quite comfortable for sea lions because they move up and down with the tides. In their natural **habitat** (on rocks or beaches) sea lions must move to higher ground when the tides roll in.

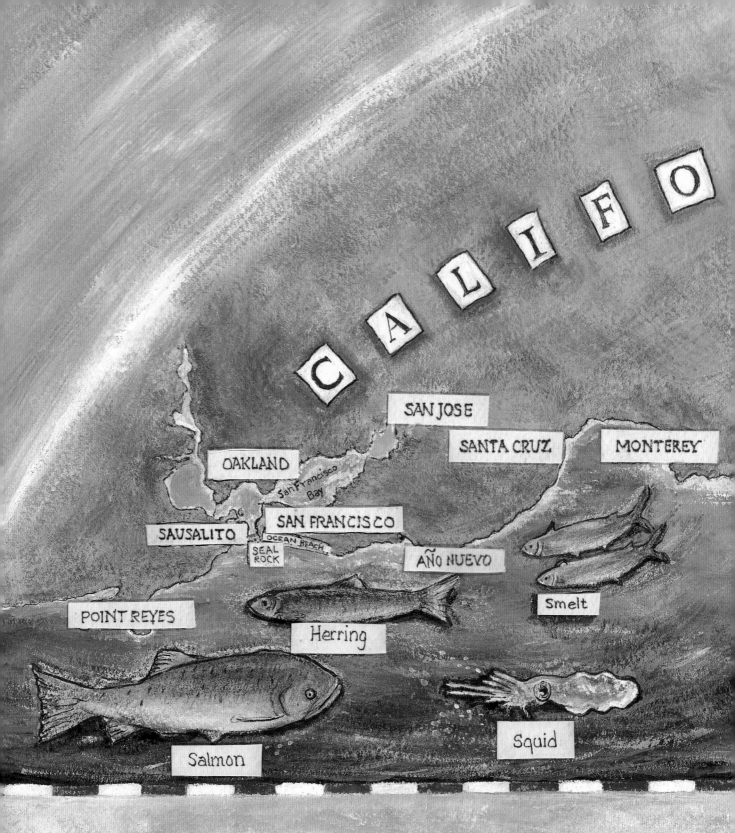

CALIFO

SAN JOSE

SANTA CRUZ   MONTEREY

OAKLAND

San Francisco Bay

SAUSALITO   SAN FRANCISCO

OCEAN BEACH

SEAL ROCK

AÑO NUEVO

Smelt

POINT REYES

Herring

Salmon

Squid

Before the sea lions came to Pier 39, they lived north of Ocean Beach at Seal Rock. Some people believe the sea lions abandoned the rocky island and relocated out of fear. A devastating earthquake shook California on October 17, 1989. The sea lions may have associated Seal Rock with danger.

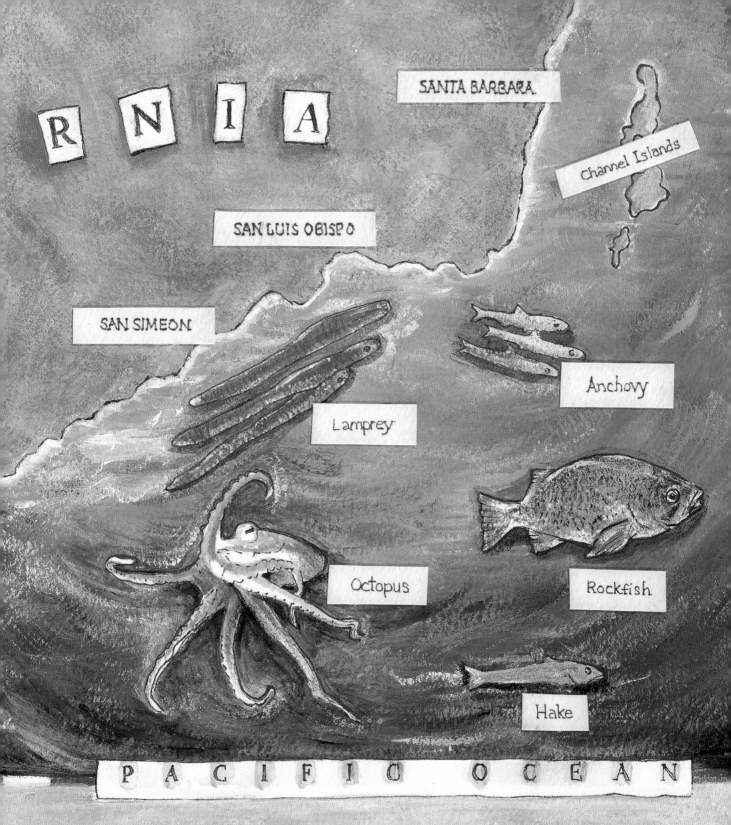

Others believe the sea lions moved to Pier 39 because of an abundance of herring in the San Francisco Bay. Sea lions eat these fish as a main part of their diet. In the winter herring are plentiful because they come to the **Bay** to lay their eggs. Sea lions also **prey** on rockfish, salmon, anchovies, smelt, lamprey, hake, squid, and octopus.

It is not known for certain if the sea lions came to Pier 39 for the herring or if they left Seal Rock because of the earthquake. All that is certain is that the population continued to grow. In January of 1990, the **colony** held a total of around 150 sea lions. By February, the number quickly reached 250. In March, there were 400 sea lions! As the population grew, San Francisco's tourists flocked to Pier 39. Visitors snapped photographs and laughed out loud at the playful **marine mammals**.

The sea lions were fun to watch at K dock, but not everyone enjoyed their company. Boat owners could not use the docks anymore because the sea lions would not move. People tried to "shoo" away the smelly mammals, but the sea lions just **barked** and ignored them. Sea lions are wild animals and can be dangerous because they are very large. Boaters had to give up their slips and move to other docks for safety.

Most of the California sea lions at Pier 39 are males. Adult males, or "bulls," can weigh up to 850 pounds and reach eight feet long. It is easy to recognize **mature** males because they are dark brown in color, have a thick neck, and have a bump called a "sagittal crest" on their forehead. Females are lighter in color and much smaller. They can weigh up to 250 pounds and reach five and a half feet long.

It is not common, but occasionally other species haul out with the California sea lions. Harbor seals have been seen on K dock on a few rare occasions. They are smaller than sea lions and keep their distance by hauling out away from the group. A male Steller sea lion named "Huey" has made several appearances at Pier 39. He is bigger than the other sea lions but they do not appear to be intimidated by his size. Young males have been seen piled up and resting on top of him!

Young males at Pier 39 are constantly barking loudly and pushing each other off the docks. They appear to be "arguing" and fighting all the time. When they do this they are not really trying to hurt each other. They are practice-fighting so that when they mature they can defend their **breeding territories** from other males. As adults they will fight for the best spot on the beach near the most females.

Just as quickly as the sea lions came to Pier 39, they began to leave. At the beginning of June 1990, almost all the sea lions left K dock. It was **breeding season** so the sea lions went to their **rookeries**. The main rookery is 370 miles away from Pier 39 in the Channel Islands. At that time people did not know whether or not the sea lions would return to San Francisco after breeding season.

Females stay close to the rookeries all year round to care for their young "pups." Sea lions have an eleven-month **gestation**, including a special ability to delay the growth of the **embryo** for up to three months. In May or June, each female gives birth to one pup weighing between 12 and 14 pounds. Pups nurse from their mothers for up to one year. They eat fish, in addition to their mother's milk, when they reach two months of age.

When pups are too young to swim, their mothers leave them on land while they hunt in the ocean. While the mothers are away, the pups will gather together for safety. They splash and play in shallow water with "toys" like seaweed and fish. They also play-fight, blow bubbles in the water, and rest on top of one another.

Sea lion pups are never seen at Pier 39. They are not able to swim the long distance from the rookeries to Pier 39. Adult sea lions can stay underwater for up to fifteen minutes and swim up to twenty-five miles per hour. They conserve energy by swimming much slower for long journeys. They can increase their speed by **porpoising** out of the water as they swim.

Sea lions are mammals, so they cannot breathe underwater like fish. Mammals, fish, and all living things need **oxygen** to survive. Oxygen is found in the air and in the water. In the water, fish filter oxygen through their **gills**. On land, sea lions and all mammals breathe air through their lungs. That is why fish cannot breathe out of water and sea lions will drown if they are underwater too long.

In July of 1990, the sea lions had been gone from Pier 39 for about two months. Breeding season was over. Were the sea lions going to come back to San Francisco? The answer was evident in August when a few sea lions arrived back at Pier 39. By mid-October, around 100 sea lions had returned and there were 500 by January of 1991. The sea lions had returned to their "home" in San Francisco.

When sea lions leave San Francisco Bay to **migrate** to their rookeries, they must travel through the Pacific Ocean. This is very dangerous for them. Ocean **predators**, such as great white sharks and orcas, continuously pose a deadly threat. In the Bay, they are safe from their natural predators. Great white sharks and orcas do not come into the Bay.

Sea lions are very curious and playful. Unfortunately they play with **plastic debris** like ribbons, ropes, fishing lines, nets, and plastic strapping. Sometimes they end up getting tangled in it. Sea lions have very sensitive whiskers that enable them to detect objects in the water. They could avoid the debris if they could only determine that it is dangerous.

"Flea Collar" was one of the first sea lions to arrive at Pier 39. He was a large male California sea lion. He got his name because a piece of plastic strapping which looked like a flea collar was tangled around his neck. Many mammals and other species like birds and sea turtles are hurt or killed by swallowing or becoming tangled in man-made debris.

When sea lions like Flea Collar are hurt or sick in the wild, volunteers from organizations like The Marine Mammal Center try to help them. They help by giving them medicine and removing plastic rings and nets from their necks. When they get better, they are released back to the wild. The Center's staff and team of volunteers have successfully rescued, rehabilitated, and released many sick and injured sea lions.

One such sea lion, named "Bingo," had a piece of fishing line tangled around his neck. When rescuers found him they approached very quietly, crouched behind **herding boards**, and slowly surrounded him. When they got close enough they "scooted" him into an animal carrier using a large net. Bingo's condition was very serious. He was transported to The Center's animal hospital in Sausalito, California.

Rescuers have a very difficult and dangerous job because sea lions are **instinctively** afraid of people. They become quite alert and aggressive when they sense danger. In order to protect themselves animals will either fight or flee from their predators. If they are near water they will avoid being captured by jumping in and swimming away. If they are on land and are too weak to swim, they may try to bite. This survival instinct is called "fight or flight."

Bingo was lucky in a sense because he was very weak when rescuers found him. Had he been more alert or surrounded by healthy sea lions, it would have been too dangerous for team members to attempt a rescue. The Center's staff and volunteers go to great lengths to minimize human/animal contact. They "hide" behind herding boards during rescues and put up screens in the hospital to shield caregivers from the animals' view. They do this so the animals won't become **tame** during their hospital stay.

When Bingo arrived at the hospital a veterinarian assessed his injuries. The fishing net had cut into his **blubber** and severed the air tube in his throat. His injuries made it nearly impossible for him to breathe. The veterinarian performed surgery on him and saved his life. When he recovered he was released back into the ocean. After Bingo's release, he was identified at Pier 39. His **Reise tag** number along with the unique scar under his chin confirmed his identity.

PIER 39

HARASSMENT OF
SEA LIONS IS
A VIOLATION OF
THE MARINE
MAMMAL
PROTECTION ACT
——————————
NO DOCKING

The Marine Mammal Center continuously monitors the sea lion colony at Pier 39. Volunteers and staff members check for Reise tags, **marks**, injured sea lions, and other marine mammal species like harbor seals and Steller sea lions, and count how many sea lions are at Pier 39 every day. This information is used to track former hospital patients, record population dynamics, and study interactions with other species.

While at Pier 39, visitors may see sea lions in a **raft** or colony holding up their flippers. It might look like they are waving, but actually they do this to cool down. Blood flowing through their flippers cools quicker when it is exposed to air. Flippers also have no blubber, so heat can escape through their skin.

No one knows for certain why hundreds of sea lions decided to move to Pier 39. Since they are safe from their ocean predators, have an abundance of prey, and have a convenient place to haul out, it is no mystery why they choose to stay. Judging by their growing numbers, it appears the sea lions won't be leaving San Francisco anytime soon.

GLOSSARY

Bark: sea lion vocalization

Bay: a part of the sea confined by land

Blubber: thick layer of fat under a sea lion's skin

Breeding season: time of year when sea lions mate

Breeding territory: section of land established and defended by bulls during breeding season

Colony: group of sea lions living together

Embryo: an animal growing in its mother's womb

Gestation: period of time an embryo spends in the mother's womb

Gills: respiratory organs of fish

Gregarious: living or traveling in a group

Habitat: natural residence of a plant or animal

Hauling out: to rest on land

Herding boards: wooden shields used to minimize human/animal contact

Instinctively (instinct): refers to an act an animal performs that is not learned; for example, building a nest, nursing young, or defending territories

Marine mammal: warm-blooded animal that lives in the ocean

Marks: identification methods and devices for marine mammals, including brands, dyes, radio tags, and time depth recorders

Mature: to grow older

Migrate: to travel to another place for a specific period of the year

Oxygen: gaseous element found in the air and water that is essential for plant and animal respiration

Plastic debris: man-made materials made out of plastic, including ribbons, fishing lines, six-pack rings, nets, ropes, and straps from packages

Porpoising: act of leaping out of the water while continuing to swim

Predator: animal that eats other animals

Prey: animals that are eaten by other animals

Raft: group of sea lions resting together while floating on the water's surface

Reise tags: plastic, color-coded, numbered tags used to identify individual animals

Rookery: sandy beach that is used by sea lions for breeding, giving birth, and caring for pups

Tame: when an animal loses its wildness

about
THE MARINE MAMMAL CENTER

The Marine Mammal Center is a nonprofit hospital dedicated to the care of wild marine mammals. The Center helps animals that are sick, injured, or orphaned along 600 miles of California's northern and central coastline. Some mammals that The Center treats are endangered species. Since 1975, over 9,000 marine mammals have received a second chance at life. Thousands of rescued animals... like Bingo, have been successfully treated and released back to the ocean. The Center rescues sea lions, seals, sea otters, whales, dolphins, and porpoises. Sea turtles, although not mammals, receive help as well.

The Center's staff helps marine mammals by treating, studying, and educating people about them. By treating them, veterinarians save animals and learn important information about their health. They also study connections between the animal's health and the state of the ocean. This is important because marine mammals, as well as all life on earth, are directly affected by the health of the ocean. Pollution, debris, and the balance between prey and predators are all factors that affect marine mammal populations. The Center educates students, researchers, policy makers, and others about the animals they rescue. By learning about the health of marine mammals, people can help keep the ocean safe for everyone.

Help The Marine Mammal Center respond to these amazing animals. Visit their web site at www.marinemammalcenter.org to learn more about this organization.

The
Marine Mammal
Center™
Advancing Rehabilitation,
Scientific Discovery and Education